60 Cast Iron Skillet Recipes

Billy Dunklin

Copyright © 2016 Billy Dunklin

All rights reserved. No part of this publication may be reproduced, distributed, or transmitted in any form or by any means, including photocopying, recording, or other electronic or mechanical methods, without the prior written permission of the publisher, except in the case of brief quotations embodied in critical reviews and certain other noncommercial uses permitted by copyright law.

Limit of Liability

The information in this book is solely for informational purposes, not as a medical instruction to replace the advice of your physician or as a replacement for any treatment prescribed by your physician. The author and publisher do not take responsibility for any possible consequences from any treatment, procedure, exercise, dietary modification, action or application of medication which results from reading or following the information contained in this book.

If you are ill or suspect that you have a medical problem, we strongly encourage you to consult your medical, health, or other competent professional before adopting any of the suggestions in this book or drawing inferences from it.

This book and the author's opinions are solely for informational and educational purposes. The author specifically disclaims all responsibility for any liability, loss, or risk, personal or otherwise which is incurred as a consequence, directly or indirectly, of the use and application of any of the contents of this book.

ISBN-13: 978-1530187232

ISBN-10: 1530187230

DEDICATION

To all who desire to live life to the fullest!

TABLE OF CONTENT

INTRODUCTION 1

Choice of your cast iron skillet: 2

Advantages: 3

Chicken Sausage with potatoes and sauerkraut 5

Chicken pad Thai... 6

Chicken and Kale Pizza Bake 8

Marinated Grilled Chicken Breasts 9

   Roasted Lemon Herb Chicken 11

Three Cheese Mac & Cheese 12

Splayed Roast Chicken with Caramelized Ramps 14

Broiled Shrimp with Tomatoes and White Beans......... 16

Gnocchi and Chickpea Skillet Dinner 17

Italian Style Halibut with Sage 18

Chicken-and-Wild Rice Casserole 20

Baked Penne with Roasted Vegetables......................... 21

Ravioli Lasagna Recipe 23

Cast-Iron Cowboy Steak.. 24

Skillet Lasagna... 26

Pasta primavera:... 27

Garlic Parmesan Cream Sauce over Pasta 29

Baked Fish with Parmesan-Sour Cream Sauce 30

Pan Fried Pork Chops 31

Creamless Penne Pasta Primavera with Olive Oil and Garlic 32

Baked Pasta with Sausage, Tomatoes, and Cheese 34

Seared scallops with lemon and vodka 36

Argentine chimichurri sauce 37

Baked Penne with Roasted Vegetables 38

Whole Grain Lasagne with Roasted Zucchini, Spicy Marinara Sauce & Ricotta Cheese 41

Seared scallops with lemon and oregano 42

Turkey and Vegetable Skillet 44

Ginger & chicken noodles 45

Salt & pepper turkey 47

Sautéed Broccoli Rabe 49

Pan-Fried Beef Tenderloin 50

Turkey skillet dinner 51

Turkey Breast Roast with Garlic, Paprika and black pepper 53

Skillet Orecchiette with Sausage and Broccoli Rabe 54

One- Skillet Bean & Broccoli Rabe Supper 56

Skillet Beef Stew 58

Broccoli Rabe and Chicken Sandwich Recipe 60

Beef and Vegetable Skillet 61

Easy Pan-Roasted Chicken Breasts with Bourbon-Mustard Pan Sauce 63

Pasta e Ceci 65

Beef and Vegetable Skillet 66

One-Pan Orecchiette with Chickpeas and Olives 68

Chicken Spinach Roulade 69

Creole Rice Skillet with Andouille Sausage 71

Roasted Chili, Garlic & Lime Chicken Quesadillas 72

Beef stew 73

5-Minute Guacamole 76

Home-style Beef Stew 77

Spring Vegetable Skillet 78

Zucchini, Brie & Caramelized Onion Panini 79

Honey Sriracha Skillet Pork Chops 81

Chicken Barley Soup 82

Paprika Chicken Salad 84

Shaved Beet & Carrot Salad with Spicy-Sweet Dressing 85

Roasted Sweet Potato and Quinoa Soup 86

Cast-Iron Carrots with Curry 87

Skillet Chicken with Bacon and White Wine Sauce 89

Pan-Seared Filet Mignon with Cabernet Sauce 91

Fajita with Roasted Chili Garlic and Lime Skillet Sauce 92

Steamed Oysters with Smokey Peach Sauce................ 93

INTRODUCTION

You are privileged to have got this book of irresistible dinner recipes at your disposal. Congrats. Introducing you to CAST IRON SKILLET RECIPES this book will be of tremendous help in preparing your meals.

Know more about your Cast Iron Skillets:

But versatile cast iron goes from stovetop to oven to grill with ease that you can bake a cake in it as well as fry unbelievably crisp catfish. It boost your reputation as a savvy cook

Apart from being an ideal heat conductor, cast iron pan heats evenly and consistently, it is inexpensive and will last a lifetime with proper care'. It is an old-fashioned way to cook fat free.

When well seasoned, a cast iron pan will be stick resistant.

Cast iron cookwares are precision cooking tools, they are dependable pans and able to control the cooking temperature. The retention of the heat of these pans allow for even cooking temperature with no hot spots, cast iron pans can be used on stove top or to bake in the oven. Its well worth the time and money to invest in one;

A frying pan or skillet is a flat-bottomed pan used for frying, searing, and browning foods. It is typically (8 to 12 inches) in diameter with relatively low sides that flare outward frypan.

A skillet has sides that flare outward at an angle. It is a versatile pan that combines the best of both the sauté pan and the frying pan has higher, sloping sides that are often slightly curved. Because of its straight sides, a 12-inch sauté pan will also have a large, twelve inch wide cooking surface.

A skillet loses at least an inch on each side, making the effective cooking area only 10-inches wide. The lighter weight of a skillet makes it superior for shaking and stirring to promote even cooking of vegetables or pieces of chopped meat. The sloping sides of a skillet allow you to easily shake the pan, performing the jump-flip maneuver that cooks like to show off 12-inch skillet with a 10-inch cooking area will sear foods more efficiently. The slanted sides make this pan perfect for stir-frying and quick cooking techniques.

Choice of your cast iron skillet:

Choose the one that is comfortable for you preferably 10-inch- 12-inch cast iron skillet will be ideal.

Care of cast iron skillet:

1. Always pre heat your cast iron before you use it.

2. Seasoning or curing is a trick to maintaining your cast iron skillet; this will not allow your food to stick.

3. Do not use hard object to scrub your cast iron skillets for this might alter its coatings.

4. You can use vegetable oil to season it and do that when it is warm.

Why you should you season your cast iron skillets:

1. It will prevent your meal from sticking to the bottom of your pan.

2. You will be filling the pores and voids in the metal with grease, which is later cooked in so providing a smooth non-stick surface in the pan.

3. It creates a non- sticky cookware.

4. It brings back old cast iron pan as a new one.

5. To create a slick and glassy coating by baking on a several thin coats of oil.

Advantages:

1. It is easy to maintain.

2. It gives your meals fragrance.

3. Its durability is of great advantage to the users.

Cast Iron Skillets are the most essential utensils needed in our kitchen. Cast iron skillet is an old fashioned kitchen utensil that our mothers used in their own time. By the time you compare it to the other kitchen utensils used now a day, you will agree with me that Cast iron skillets beat them all.

Chicken Sausage with potatoes and sauerkraut

Preparation: 30 minutes

Ingredients:

1 tbsp of extra-virgin olive oil

12 oz (4 links) chicken sausage (cooked), lengthwise (halved) and

 Cut into 2- 3-inch pieces

1 medium onion (sliced thinly)

3 medium Yukon Gold potatoes, halved and

Cut into 1/4-inch (slices)

1 1/2 cups of (rinsed) sauerkraut

1 1/2 cups of white wine (dry)

1/2 tsp of ground pepper (freshly)

1/4 tsp of caraway seeds

1 bay leaf

Directions:

1. Heat the oil in a large skillet over a medium heat.

2. Add the sausage and the onion then cook, mix continually until it begins to brown for about 4 min.

3. Add the potatoes, the sauerkraut, wine, the pepper, the caraway seeds and the bay leaf;

4. Heat, covered with a lid and cook. Stir occasionally till potatoes are all tender and most of it liquid is evaporated or for about ten -fifteen minutes. Take away the bay leaf before you serve

Chicken pad Thai

Ingredients:

8 ounce of rice noodles

1/4 cup of salted peanuts (chopped)

1/2 teaspoons freshly zest lime peel

3 tablespoons of fish sauce

2 tablespoons of fresh lime (juice)

2 tablespoons of packed dark brown sugar

4 1/2 teaspoons of rice vinegar

1 tablespoon of siracha

3 tablespoons of vegetable oil

1 pound of boneless, skinless chicken breasts, cut into bite size strips

6 garlic cloves (minced)

1 egg, lightly beaten

1 cup of bean sprouts (fresh)

1/2 cup of scallions, sliced

2 tablespoons of cilantro (fresh and snipped)

Directions:

1. Place noodles in a large bowl.

2. Add hot water to it and cover and let remain there for about ten – fifteen minutes until flexible, but not soft.

3. Remove the water and put aside.

4. Then mix the peanuts and lime peel; set aside.

5. Mix together the fish sauce, lime juice, brown sugar, rice vinegar, and chili sauce in a bowl.

6. Heat one tablespoon of oil in a pan over medium-high heat then add the chicken and garlic; cook and stir until chicken is no longer pink.

7. Transfer it to a bowl and put it aside.

8. Add egg to hot skillet and cook for about 30 seconds.

9. Then turn the egg with spoon and cook for about 30 seconds more, until it is ready.

10. Heat the remaining two tablespoons of oil over high heat for about 30 seconds.

11. Add the drained noodles and the bean sprouts, then mix and cook for about two minutes.

12. Add the fish sauce mixture and chicken to the skillet and cook for about 1 - 2 minutes. You garnish with egg, peanuts, scallions, and fresh cilantro in a plate.

Chicken and Kale Pizza Bake

Ingredients:

Olive oil

Salt and pepper (to taste)

4. Chicken breasts (boneless) cut in half

1 bunch kale, remove the centre stalks, cut into thin ribbons

2 teaspoons of oregano

1½ cups of pizza sauce

1 of cup shredded mozzarella cheese (partly skimmed)

Directions:

1. Preheat the oven to 375°F

2. Heat a good glug of olive oil in a large skillet set over medium heat.

3. Both sides of the chicken breast should be seasoned with salt and pepper,

4. The skin side of the chicken breast should be placed in the pan and cook until golden brown for about four minutes.

5. Turn the other side and cook for about 2mins.

6. Then remove it from the pan and put the meat in a plate.

7. Add another glug of oil to the pan and sauté the kale until wilted for about five minutes.

8. Season it lightly with some salt and pepper (as desired) and mix to combine.

9. The chicken and its juices to be put back in the pan with the kale pressed (nestled) together.

10. Sprinkle the oregano over top, then mix the pizza sauce with ½ cup water and pour it over the chicken and kale.

11. Top with the shredded mozzarella and bake at 375°F for about 20mins, or till the cheese is golden brown and bubbling.

Marinated Grilled Chicken Breasts

Preparation time: 20 minutes

Cooking time: 10 minutes

Ingredients:

1/2 cup of soy sauce (use gluten-free soy sauce for GF option)

1/3 cup of olive oil

Juice from one large lemon

2 tbsp of honey

1 tbsp of garlic salt

1 tsp of oregano

6 chicken breasts (boneless, skinless)

Directions:

1. Mix the ingredients 1-6 in a bowl.

2. The marinade and the chicken breasts should be added into a large zip top bag.

3. Tie the bag and press the meat from the outside of the bag in order to have each of them coated with marinade.

4. Allow the chicken to rest on the counter top for about thirty minutes.

5. Heat the grill or grill pan to medium heat.

6. Spray a paper towel with non-stick spray, using tongs; rub the grill with the paper towel.

7. Put the chicken on top of the grill and cook each side for about five-eight minutes until the chicken is cooked thoroughly and no longer pink.

8. Allow the chicken to rest on a plate or platter for five minutes after you have removed it from the heat.

Roasted Lemon Herb Chicken

Ingredients:

2 tsp of Italian seasoning

1/2 tsp of seasoning salt

1/2 tsp of mustard powder

1 tsp of powder garlic

1/2 tsp of black pepper ground

1 (3 lb) whole chicken

2 lemons

2 tbsp of olive oil

Directions:

1. Preheat oven to 350 degrees F.

2. Mix the salt, mustard powder, garlic powder and black pepper and put it aside.

3. Wash the chicken very well and remove the giblets.

4. Place the chicken in a 9 by 13 inch baking dish.

5. Spread 1 1/2 tsp of the spice mixture inside the chicken.

6. Use the remaining mixture and rub on the body of the chicken.

7. Squeeze out the juice of the lemons into a small bowl and stir with the olive oil.

8. Pour slowly the oil and juice mixture over the chicken.

9. Bake it in the oven you have preheated for 1 1/2 hours, or until juices is not there, basting continually with the remaining oil mixture.

Three Cheese Mac & Cheese

Cooking time: 25 min

Ingredients:

¾ 1b of penne

1½ cups of heavy cream

3 tbsp of yellow onion (finely chopped)

2 minced garlic cloves

2 tbsp of all purpose flour

5 oz of goat cheese

3 oz of shredded sharp white cheddar

½ cup of packed grated parmesan (freshly)

2 tbsp of sour cream

¾ tsp of zest lemon

1½ of tsp fresh chopped thyme

Salt and ground white/black pepper freshly

An extra large of egg yolk

Directions:

1. Heat the oven to 400°. Rub inside a cast-iron skillet of 10-inch in size with butter. Cook the pasta in a big pot of boiling salted water until all is soft.

2. Remove the water from the pasta and return to pot, and then simmer the heavy cream, the garlic and onion in a big saucepan.

3. Put in ½ cup of the cream into a medium bowl then gently mix in the flour; then return the mixture in to the saucepan.

4. Take away the bowl and continue the mixing over an average heat until it is thick, for three minutes.

5. Take it away from the heat and add the goat cheese, the cheddar and the half of the Parmesan until it melts, then mix in the sour cream, the zest and one tsp of thyme and then season it with the desired salt and pepper.

6. Put in the yolk of egg in a small bowl then steadily mix ½ cup of cheese sauce into it.

7. Steadily mix the egg mixture in the saucepan then pour in the cheese sauce on the pasta and shake it to coat it evenly.

8. Add pasta to cast-iron skillet and sprinkle with remaining cheese.

Then bake for twenty to twenty-five minutes, until bubbling and golden brown. Sprinkle with remaining thyme. Allow Mac and Cheese to rest for five minutes.

Splayed Roast Chicken with Caramelized Ramps

Ingredients:

1 4 1/2-1b whole chicken, (patted dry)

2 tsp of kosher salt

½ tsp of ground black pepper (freshly)

1 bunch of fresh ramps (6 oz)

1 lemon, (quartered)

1 tbsp extra virgin of olive oil

5 garlic cloves, (smashed and peeled)

1 tbsp capers

Directions:

1. Rub the chicken inside and out with salt and pepper, two to three hours ahead and refrigerate it uncovered (that is if the time is on your side). If not, let it rest uncovered at room temperature while the oven heats.

2. Place a big cast-iron skillet in the oven and heat to 500 degrees for about forty-five minutes. If you salted the chicken in advance, take it out of the fridge so it can warm to room temperature.

3. Meanwhile, prep the ramps: trim the hairy bottoms and remove the outer layer of the skin. Remove the leaves from the bulbs, rinse them gently, and clean it dry. Cut the any fat bulbs (wider than a pencil) in half lengthwise. Cut the leaves into large pieces.

4. Cut the skin connecting the legs to the body. Splay the thighs open until you feel the joint pop on each side. Place 2 lemon wedges inside the chicken.

5. Carefully transfer the chicken, breast-side up, to the hot skillet, Press down on the legs so they rest flat on the bottom of the pan.

6. Slowly pour the oil on the bird.

7. Roast for about thirty minutes. Mix the ramp bulbs (not leaves) garlic and capers into the skillet.

8. Turn to coat them with pan juices then roast for about five minutes, and then turn again. Continue the cooking until the ramps are soft and chicken is no longer pink, five to fifteen minutes more.

9. Remove the chicken from oven and stir the ramp leaves into the pan until is wilted. The chicken should be left to rest for about five min, then serve with the pan juices and ramps

Broiled Shrimp with Tomatoes and White Beans

Ingredients:

2 cups of grape tomatoes (12 oz)

1 can (19 oz) of white beans, (drained and rinsed)

2 tbsp of brine-packed capers to be rinsed

1 tbsp of minced garlic (from 4 cloves)

2 tbsp of extra-virgin olive oil, and more for drizzling

Coarse salt

1 1b of shelled large shrimp (preferably 15), with the tails intact

3/4 cup of chicken stock

Directions:

1. Heat the broiler. Preheat a large, heavy cast iron skillet on top of the rack for about fifteen minutes.

2. Then mix the tomatoes, beans, capers, garlic with one tbsp of oil with 1/2 tsp of salt together in a bowl.

3. Mix the shrimp with the remaining tbsp of oil and 1/4 tsp of salt in another bowl.

4. Remove the skillet from the oven then add the tomato mixture.

5. Cook until tomatoes are charred and beginning to collapse, for five minutes.

6. Remove from the oven and stir in stock, then shrimp.

7. Cook stirring halfway through, until shrimps is opaque for about three minutes. Pour in the oil slowly

Gnocchi and Chickpea Skillet Dinner

Ingredients:

1 package (16 - 18 oz) of gnocchi

2 tablespoon of butter

2 cloves garlic, (crushed)

4 strips of turkey bacon, (diced)

1 teaspoon of oregano

1 teaspoon of basil

1 cup of mushrooms, (sliced)

1 small head of broccoli crowns, (chopped)

1 can (19 oz) of chickpeas, (drained and rinsed)

Directions:

1. Cook gnocchi in boiling water until they float to the top, then remove the water and put aside.

2. Melt the butter in a large non-stick skillet, over medium heat.

3. Sauté the garlic for about one minute, then adds the gnocchi and bacon, and cook for about five minutes until they are slightly brown.

4. Put the remaining ingredients, cover the skillet, and cook for another fifteen minutes on a medium-low heat, stirring it occasionally

Italian Style Halibut with Sage

Ingredients:

1 tbsp of olive oil

1 (1-1b) of halibut filet, (cut into 4 equal pieces)

1 large yellow onion, (thinly sliced)

2 cloves garlic, (minced)

1 (14 1/2-oz) can diced tomatoes

1 (9-oz) can cannellini beans, (thoroughly rinsed and drained)

1 (12-oz) jar of roasted red peppers (drained and sliced)

3 tbsp chopped (fresh sage) or (1 tbsp dried)

1 tsp of kosher salt

Black pepper (freshly ground)

Directions:

1. Heat the olive oil in a 12-inch skillet over medium high heat.

2. Sear the halibut until golden brown, four - six minutes on each side.

3. Remove it from the pan and put it aside then add onions and garlic to the pan, and sauté until softened enough to your taste, for five – 7 seven minutes.

4. Add tomatoes, beans, and red peppers; mix to combine. Nestle halibut into the pan cook until the fish is flaky and cooked all the way through, for ten – fifteen minutes. Stir in sage, salt, and pepper to taste.

Chicken-and-Wild Rice Casserole

Cooking time: 1 Hour 15 Minutes

Ingredients:

1 (2.25-oz) package of sliced almonds

2 (6.2-ounces) boxes of fast-cooking long-grain and wild rice mix

1/4 cup of butter

4 celery ribs, (chopped)

2 medium Onion (chopped)

5 cups of chopped cooked chicken

2 (10 3/4-ounces) cans of cream of mushroom soup

2 (8-ounces) cans of chopped water chestnuts (drained)

1 (8-ounces) container of sour cream

1 cup of milk

1/2 tsp of salt

1/2 tsp of pepper

4 cups (16 ounces) of shredded Cheddar cheese (divided)

2 cups of soft breadcrumbs (fresh)

Directions:

1. Preheat oven to 350°and bake the almonds in a single layer in a shallow pan for about four to six minutes or till toasted and fragrant, mixing it halfway through.

2. Prepare the rice mixes as directed on package.

3. Then, melt the butter in a large skillet over medium heat; add the celery and the onions. Sauté for about 10 minutes or until it is soft.

4. Stir in the chicken, the cream of mushroom soup, chopped water chestnuts (drained) sour cream, milk, salt and pepper to taste as desired rice, and 3 cups of cheese.

Spoon the mixture into a lightly greased 15- by 10-inch baking dish then top it with breadcrumbs.

5. Bake it at 350°F for about 35 min then sprinkle on it with the remaining cup of cheese, and top it with the toasted almonds bake for about 5 min

Baked Penne with Roasted Vegetables

Preparation time: 25min

Cooking time: 40min

Ingredients:

2 red peppers (in strips 2cm in width)

2 zucchini (lengthwise, quartered) in 2cm cubes

2 summer squash, (lengthwise, quartered) and cut into 2cm cubes

4 (halved) button of mushrooms (halved)

1 yellow onion, (peel and slice) into strips, 2cm in size

4 tbsp of extra-virgin olive oil,

1 teaspoon of salt, divided,

1 teaspoon of black pepper ground (freshly), divided,

1 tablespoon of dried Italian herb mix or herbs de Provence,

500 g of penne pasta,

120 g of grated fontina cheese,

750 ml of marinara sauce homemade or bought,

60 g of smoked mozzarella, grated

220 g of frozen peas, (thawed)

30 g of grated Parmesan, plus 30g to top it,

30 g of butter (cut in pieces)

Directions:

1. Preheat the oven to 220°C/gas mark.

2. Mix the peppers, the zucchini, the squash, the mushrooms, and the onions with olive oil, 1/2 tsp of salt, 1/2 tsp of pepper, and the dried herbs.

3. Roast them till tender for 15 min boil salted water in a large pot over a high heat.

4. Add the pasta and cook for 6 min. (Let it still be strong a bit because it will still be re cooked the second time in the oven) Drain it in a colander.

5. In a large bowl, mix the drained pasta with the roasted vegetables, the marinara sauce, then cheeses, the peas, 1/2 tsp of salt, and 1/2 tsp of pepper use a wooden spoon, to mix it gently till all the pasta is well rubbed with the sauce and the other ingredients are well combined.

6. Put the pasta into a greased pan of size 23-cm x 33-cm, then top it with the remaining 30g Parmesan and the butter pieces. Bake it until the top is golden and the cheese melts, for 25mins.

Ravioli Lasagna Recipe

Ingredients:

1 1b of ground beef

1 jar (28 oz) of spaghetti sauce

1 package (25 oz) of frozen sausage or cheese ravioli

1-1/2 cups (6 oz) of shredded part-skim mozzarella cheese

Directions:

1. Cook the beef in a large skillet over medium heat until no longer pink; then remove the water it.

2. Grease a 2-1/2-qt. baking dish, layer 1/3 of the spaghetti sauce,

1/2 of the ravioli and beef and 1/2 cup of cheese; repeat the layers.

3. Top it with the remaining sauce and cheese.

4. Cover and bake at 400° for 40-45 min or till heated through.

Cast-Iron Cowboy Steak

Ingredients:

Black pepper ground (fresh) and Kosher salt

1 (1 1/2- to 2-Pounds) bone-in rib-eye or porterhouse steak (2 inch in thickness)

1 tbsp of vegetable oil

3 tbsp of butter

8 herb sprigs (oregano, rosemary and thyme)

3 cloves garlic, peeled then smashed

Directions:

1. Preheat grill to 400° to 450° a high heat.

2. A 12-inch cast-iron skillet is placed on grill then heats it; cover it with grill lid for, 15 minutes.

3. Sprinkle salt and pepper generously over steak (to your taste).

4. Put oil into the skillet. (Heat the Oil very well till it smokes) Use tongs, place the steak in the skillet, and cook on the grill, with no lid, for 10 min or until it is dark brown and also crusty.

5. Turn the steak on the fatty edge in the skillet, holding upright with tongs, and cook two for minutes.

6. Put the steak, the uncooked side down, in the skillet.

7. Cook on the grill and cover with a grill lid, 8 - 10 min. Temperature of 120° to 125° for medium-rare; temperature will rise as the steak rests.

8. Mix the butter, the herbs, and the garlic to the side of the skillet, then cook for2 - 3 min or till the butter begins to foam.

9. Slightly tilt your skillet, and spoon butter mixture over the steak between 20 times (be careful). Place the steak, the herbs, and the garlic into a plate; leave it for about 5 to 10 min. Slice against the grain.

Skillet Lasagna

Cooking time: 30mins.

Ingredients:

3/4 1b of beef (ground)

2 garlic cloves,(minced)

(14-1/2 oz can of diced tomatoes with basil, oregano and garlic, undrained

2 jars (14 oz each) of spaghetti sauce

2/3 cup of condensed cream of onion soup, (undiluted)

2 eggs, lightly beaten

1-1/4 cups of cottage cheese (1%)

3/4 tsp of Italian seasoning

9 lasagna noodles

1/2 cup of shredded Colby-Monterey Jac (cheese)

1/2 cup of shredded part-skim mozzarella cheese

Directions:

1. Cook the beef and garlic in a large skillet over a medium heat until the meat changes color; then drain.

2. Mix in the tomatoes and the spaghetti sauce; then heat it through, to be transferred into a bowl.

3. Mix the soup, the eggs, the cottage cheese and the Italian seasoning in a smaller bowl

4. Return one cup of the meat sauce to the skillet and spread it evenly.

5. Layer with one cup of cottage cheese mixture, 1-1/2 cups of meat sauce and half of the noodles, break it as desired.

6. Repeat the layers of the cottage cheese mixture, the meat sauce and the noodles to and top with the remaining meat sauce. Boil it then reduce the heat;

7. Cover it and simmer it for about 15 - 17 min or till the noodles are tender.

8. Take it away from the heat, Sprinkle with the shredded cheeses, leave covered, allow it remain for sometime till it melts for about 2mins.

Pasta primavera:

Ingredients:

2 cups of broccoli florets

1 cup of sliced mushrooms

1 cup of sliced zucchini or yellow squash

2 cups of sliced red or green peppers

1 tbsp of extra-virgin olive oil

1/2 cup of chopped onion

2 garlic cloves, minced

1 tsp of butter

1 cup of evaporated fat-free milk

3/4 cup of grated Parmesan cheese (freshly)

12 oz whole-wheat pasta (angel hair or spaghetti)

1/3 cup of chopped fresh parsley (freshly)

Directions:

1. In a large pot fitted with a steamer basket, boil about one inch of water

2. Mix 1, 2, 3 and 4 together Cover and steam until tender-crisp, for about ten minutes.

3. Remove from pot heat the olive oil and sauté the onion and garlic in a large sauce pot over medium heat.

4. Add the steamed vegetables and stir to coat the vegetables with the onion and garlic mixture then remove from heat but keep warm.

5. Get another large saucepan, heat butter, and evaporated milk and Parmesan cheese.

6. Stir over average heat till thickened and heated through.

7. Stir continuously and don't scald. Remove from heat but keep warm.

8. Fill a large pot 3/4 full with water and boil.

9. Add the pasta and cook until tender for ten to twenty minutes.

10. Drain the pasta thoroughly. Top with vegetables and pour the sauce over the vegetables and pasta. Garnish with fresh parsley.

Garlic Parmesan Cream Sauce over Pasta

Ingredients:

1 Pound pasta

1 tbsp of extra virgin olive oil

3 tbsp of butter

1 tbsp of chopped garlic (or minced)

1/2 tsp of red pepper flakes (optional)

2 tbsp of flour

1 cup of milk

1 cup of chicken broth

1 -1 1/2 cup shredded parmesan cheese

Salt and pepper

4 -5 scallions of green onions (diced)

Directions:

When the pasta is half way done, start with cream sauce in a separate pot.

Mix butter, olive oil and garlic and sauté on a medium-low heat until butter is melted, then add red pepper flakes and sauté.

Stir in flour until combined. Add the milk and chicken broth and boil over a lower heat and stir until it becomes thickened.

Add parmesan and stir until it is melted. Serve over pasta, and top with green onions.

Add cooked, diced chicken (if desired)

Baked Fish with Parmesan-Sour Cream Sauce

Ingredients:

1 1b of orange roughly fillets

1 (8-oz) of container sour cream

1/4 cup of shredded Parmesan cheese

1/2 tsp of paprika

1/2 tsp of salt

1/4 tsp of pepper

2 tbsp of Italian-seasoned breadcrumbs

2 tbsp of butter or margarine, melted

Directions:

Place fillets in a single layer in a lightly greased 13 x 9 inch pan.

Stir together sour cream and next 4 ingredients; spread mixture evenly over the fillets.

Sprinkle with breadcrumbs, and drizzle with butter.

Bake at 350° for 20 to 25 minutes or until fish flakes with a fork.

Pan Fried Pork Chops

Ingredients:

1 tsp of seasoned salt

1 tsp of ground black pepper

8 pork breakfast chops

1 cup of all-purpose flour

Cayenne pepper

1/2 cup of canola oil

1 tbsp butter

Smashed new potatoes, for serving

Directions:

1. Season both sides of the pork chops with salt and pepper

2. Mix the flour and some of the cayenne, salt and black pepper. Coat each side of the pork chops in the flour mixture, and then put aside.

3. Heat the canola oil and butter in a skillet when butter melts add pork chops then fry. Drain off the excess oil.

Creamless Penne Pasta Primavera with Olive Oil and Garlic

Ingredients:

4 quarts of water

2 tbsp of sea salt or 2 tbsp salt

1 pound of penne pasta

2 cups of precooked broccoli florets

1 precooked carrot (1-inch sticks)

4 tbsp of extra virgin olive oil

1 small onion, (chopped)

1 tbsp of garlic, (minced)

1 red bell pepper (sliced)

1/2 cup of frozen green pea (thawed)

1/2 cup of frozen sweet corn, (thawed)

1 cup of beef broth (if desired) or 1 fluid oz of dry white wine

1 tsp fresh basil, (chopped)

Salt, as desired

Black pepper, to taste

Parmesan cheese (grated) or grana padano (grated), used separately.

Directions:

1. Boil 4 quarts of water with 2 tbsp salt in a big pot, cook the penne pasta to your desire as directed by the package (2.8 quarts - 2.5 liters) of water is used, but if the water is not much it will take longer time to boil once the pasta is added.

2. Precook the broccoli florets and the carrots. Boil the water for about 3-5 min and check if done with a fork. Steam the vegetables .Once it is done transfer the vegetables to ice water to stop the cooking and to preserve the bright color, then remove the water and put aside.

3. Heat the olive oil in a large skillet for about a minute or until hot then sauté the onion and the garlic until it turns lightly golden, for about three minutes.

4. Put in the vegetables and sauté till the peppers are soft, for 2 min.

5. Deglaze with beef broth (if used) or just a splash (one fluid oz) of dry white wine.

6. Put in the drained penne noodles and the basil and season as desired.

Mix it well and serve with some freshly grated Parmesan.

Baked Pasta with Sausage, Tomatoes, and Cheese

Ingredients;

1 (1 lb) of package of uncooked ziti short tube-shaped pasta

1 1b of hot turkey Italian sausage links

1 cup of chopped onion

2 cloves garlic, (minced)

1 tbsp of tomato paste

1/4 tsp of salt

1/4 tsp of black pepper

2 (14.5-oz) cans of petite-diced tomatoes (not drained)

1/4 cup of chopped basil (fresh)

Cooking spray

1 cup of (4 oz) shredded mozzarella cheese (fresh)

1 cup of (4 oz) of grated Parmesan cheese (fresh)

Directions:

1. Preheat the oven to 350°.

2. Cook the pasta as directed on the package, omitting the salt and the fat. Remove water from the pasta, and put aside.

3. Remove the casings from the sausage.

4. Cook the sausage, the onion, and the garlic in a large non-sticky skillet over a medium heat until it becomes brown.

5. Stir it until it becomes crumbled, add the tomato paste, the salt, the pepper, the tomatoes and boil.

6. Cover it and simmer on a lower heat for about ten minutes, stirring it often.

7. Mix the cooked pasta, the sausage mixture and the basil and put half of the pasta mixture in a 4-quart casserole coated with the cooking spray.

8. Pour half of mozzarella and half of the Parmesan.

9. Repeat layers and bake at 350° for about 25 mins or until it bubbles.

Seared scallops with lemon and vodka

Ingredients:

1 1b of sea scallops

1 tbsp plus 1 tsp of olive oil

2/3 cup of vodka

2 tbsp of heavy cream

1 tbsp of squeezed lemon juice (fresh)

1 tsp of grated lemon zest (finely)

2 tbsp of (finely chopped) fresh tarragon leaves

Directions:

Pat clean scallops dry with paper towels, rub it with one tsp of olive oil, and season it with salt and freshly ground black pepper.

Heat The remaining one tbsp of oil is heated in a large skillet over high heat.

When the oil shimmers, add scallops and cook on each side until golden brown, for

4mins. Serve it in a plate. Take away the skillet from the heat and add vodka carefully, scrape any browned bits from the bottom of the skillet, add it the sauce and mix together.

Return the pan to medium-low heat and add cream, lemon juice, and lemon zest; mix together.

Return the scallops and any accumulated juices to the skillet and cook until heated through, for two minutes.

Argentine chimichurri sauce

Ingredients:

2 cups of packed Italian parsley leaves (fresh)

4 medium garlic cloves (peeled and smashed)

1/4 cup of fresh packed oregano leaves (or four tsp of dried oregano)

1/4 cup of red wine vinegar

1/2 tsp of red pepper flakes

1/2 tsp kosher salt

Fresh black pepper (ground)

1 cup of extra-virgin olive oil

Directions:

1. Place parsley, vinegar, garlic, oregano, red pepper flakes, salt, and pepper (as desired) in a food processor's bowl fitted with a blade attachment.

2. Process it until it is finely chopped stopping and scraping down the sides of the bowl with a rubber spatula as needed for about one minute.

3. Add oil in a steady stream while the motor is still running. Remove traces down the sides of the bowl and allow it to mix for some time.

4. Place the sauce into an airtight container and refrigerate at least two hours or about a day for the flavors to meld. Stir and season as desired before serving.

Baked Penne with Roasted Vegetables

Preparation time: 25 min

Cooking time: 40 min

Ingredients:

2 red peppers (2cm wide strips /cored)

2 courgettes, (in 2cm cube and quartered lengthwise)

2 summer squash (in 2cm cube and quartered lengthwise)

4 button mushrooms (halved)

1 yellow onion, (peeled / sliced in 2cm strips)

4 tablespoons of extra-virgin olive oil,

1 teaspoon of salt (divided)

1 teaspoon of freshly ground black pepper, divided,

1 tablespoon of either dried Italian herb mix or herbs de Provence,

500 g of penne pasta,

120 g of fontina cheese (grated),

750 ml of marinara sauce (either homemade or store bought)

60 g of smoked mozzarella (grated)

220 g of frozen peas, (thawed)

30 g of grated Parmesan, (plus 30g for topping)

30 g of butter, cut into small pieces,

Directions:

Preheat the oven to 220°C/gas mark. Mix the 1-6 ingredients with 1/2 tsp salt ½ tsp of pepper with the dried herbs on a baking sheet. Roast until tender, for about 15 min.

Meanwhile, boil salted water in a large pot over a high heat then add the pasta and cook for 6 min

Since you will be cooking the pasta a second time in the oven, you want to make sure the inside remain hard. Put in the colander.

Put in a large bowl; toss the drained pasta, the roasted vegetables, the marinara sauce, the cheeses, the peas, 1/2 tsp of salt, and 1/2 tsp of pepper. Gently mix them with a wooden spoon, until all the pasta is coated with sauce and the ingredients are well combined.

Pour in the pasta in a greased 23 cm x 33 cm pan. Top with it 30 g Parmesan and pieces of butter. Bake until top is golden and the cheese melts, for about 25 minutes in a steady stream. Scrape down the sides of the bowl and pulse a few times to combine.

Keep the sauce into an airtight container and refrigerate at least for two hours or up to one day to allow the flavors to meld.

Whole Grain Lasagne with Roasted Zucchini, Spicy Marinara Sauce & Ricotta Cheese

Preparation time: 25 minutes

Cooking time: 30 minutes

Ingredients:

1 Box of Barilla Whole Grain Lasagne

4 tbsp of divided extra virgin olive oil

3 1bs of zucchini (sliced lengthwise)

1 tbsp of chopped thyme fresh

2 jars of Barilla Spicy Marinara

1 count (15 oz) ricotta cheese

1 cup of shredded Parmigiano-Reggiano cheese

Salt and black pepper as desired

Directions:

Preheat the oven to 425°F, then boil water in a large add salt to taste

Cook it as directed on the package. DRAIN the pasta then toss with one tbsp of olive oil then spread it on a sheet tray to cool.

Mix zucchini with the extra olive oil and the thyme in a big bowl, season it with salt and pepper (as desired)

Arrange the zucchini on a sheet tray and roast for about 15-20 min, or until it is lightly browned.

Take it away from the oven and lower the oven to 375*F

Spray a 13 x 9 lasagne dish with olive oil, and put one cup of sauce to the bottom of the pan.

Layer it with four sheets of lasagne, top it with the one cup of sauce, the ¼ of the ricotta mixture, the one tbsp of Parmigiano cheese, then one layer of roasted zucchini, this can be repeated for three other layers. Top the lasagna with the sauce that remains and the Parmigiano cheese, cover it with a foil then bake in the oven for about 25-30 min, or until internal temperature reaches 165°F.

Seared scallops with lemon and oregano

Cooking time: 30 min

Ingredients:

1/2 cup of all-purpose flour

2 tsp of seasoning salt

1/2 tsp of dried oregano

1/2 tsp of dried thyme

2 tbsp of lemon pepper

16 sea scallops, (rinsed and drained)

2 tbsp of olive oil

4 tbsp of chopped parsley (fresh) divided

4 tsp of lemon juice, divided

Directions:

1. Mix together flour, salt, oregano, thyme and lemon pepper together in a large bowl.

2. Roll the scallops in flour mixture till lightly coated on all the sides.

3. Heat the olive oil in a skillet over high heat.

4. Add four scallops into pan and sear on all the sides (two minutes for each side).

5. After turning the scallops then add one tbsp of parsley and one tsp of lemon juice.

6. The scallops are removed from the pan into a plate in the oven to keep warm.

7. You can repeat the same process for the remaining scallops.

Turkey and Vegetable Skillet

Ingredients:

2 t. of olive oil

1/2 1b of lean ground turkey

1/2 cup of onion, (diced)

2 cloves garlic, (minced)

1 cup of zucchini or summer squash, (diced)

1 cup of green beans, end trimmed (fresh)

1 cup of cherry tomatoes, halved

1/2 cup of fire roasted tomatoes

1 t. kosher salt

1/2 t. of dried basil

1/2 t. of dried oregano

1/4 t. of black pepper

Or smoked Gouda may also be used

Directions:

Preheat oven to broil. In a large oven proof skillet over medium high heat,

Heat the olive oil. When the oil is hot put in the ground turkey and break it up till small pieces.

When the turkey is almost cooked add the onion and the garlic. Cook it for a minute and then add in the rest of the vegetables.

Cook for another four to five minutes or until the vegetables are slightly softened.

Spread the shredded cheese on top of the turkey and vegetable mixture.

Put the skillet in the oven and boil it until the cheese is melted and golden brown.

Ginger & chicken noodles

Prep time: 15 min - 20 min

Cook: 15 min

Ingredients:

3 eggs

3 tablespoon of vegetable oil

4 boneless skinless chicken breast fillets

100 g root ginger (fresh), peeled and cut to small slithers

6 cloves garlic, (sliced)

2 bunch of spring onion (diagonal strips)

200 ml dry sherry or sake

600 g packs of straight-to-wok noodle

3 tablespoons of soy sauce

Directions:

1. Mix the eggs with 2 tablespoons of water.

2. One tablespoon of the oil should be heated in a large non-stick frying pan.

3. Swirl the eggs into pan and cook for about 2 minutes until it set, turn it over and cook for about 1 minute.

4. Put the omelets onto a board and, allow it cool enough to hold, then slice into strips and put aside.

5. Heat the remaining oil in a large wok and stir-fry chicken for about 5 minutes till it is brown, add ginger and the garlic, cook for some min. spread the spring onions over it. Reserve some to sprinkle on top, then the sake or sherry and noodles.

6. Mix everything properly. Pour slowly the soy, stir in the shredded omelets, sprinkle over reserved spring onions and ready to serve.

Salt & pepper turkey

Ingredients:

4½ -5.6 kg/10-12 pounds of turkey (thawed) giblets removed

1 tablespoon of black peppercorns

1 tablespoon of Maldon sea salt

1 lemon

Bay leaves, plus extra sprigs to garnish

50 g of butter, melted

10-12 rashers of streaky bacon

For the gravy

2 tablespoons of plain flour

600 ml turkeys or chicken stock

150 ml / ¼ of pint port

4 tablespoons of lingoberries preserve or cranberry sauce

2 tablespoons of wholegrain mustard

Directions:

1. Preheat the oven to 190C/gas 5/ fan 170C.

2. Wash the inside and outside of the turkey and dry well with kitchen paper.

3. Season inside the turkey with salt and pepper to taste, grind the peppercorns (coarsely) with a pestle and mortar and sprinkle the sea salt. Grate the lemon (finely) crust on top and mix thoroughly.

4. Cut the lemon into quarters and put inside the body cavity along with a few bay leaves.

5. When stuffing the turkey, stuff the neck end only, pushing it towards the breast. Don't overfill it, as the stuffing will increase while cooking. Any leftover stuffing can be shaped into walnut-sized balls and cooked around the turkey for the last half-hour. Secure the neck end flap with a small metal or wooden skewer.

6. Tie together the turkey legs with a kitchen string to give it a good shape. Weigh the turkey and calculate the cooking time at 18 minutes per 450g/1lb.

7. Put the turkey in a large roasting tin. Rub liberally all over with melted butter. Sprinkle the seasoning mix evenly over the breast and legs.

8. Cover the turkey loosely with a square of foil and roast for the calculated cooking time, basting with the pan juices hour. Half an hour before the end of the cooking time, remove the foil and untie the string. Re-tie the legs with a rasher of bacon and arrange the rest in a lattice over the breast. Place any stuffing balls around the turkey. Spoon off six tbsp of pan juices into a saucepan for the gravy, then return the turkey to the oven.

After the cooking transfer the turkey to a serving platter. Cover tightly with foil and leave it to rest for 15-45 minutes.

9. Then, make the gravy. Heat the six tablespoons of pan juices in the saucepan. Mix in the flour and cook for 3 min until it becomes golden. Gradually whisk in the turkey or chicken stock and port, cooking until the gravy is no longer lumpy. Stir in the lingo berry preserve (or cranberry sauce) and mustard and simmer for 5 minutes. Then taste the gravy and season (if desired).

L0. Get rid of the fat from the juices in the roasting tin; add about 150 ml /1⁄4 pint of the pan juices to the gravy. Heat through then transfer to a warmed gravy boat.

Sautéed Broccoli Rabe

Ingredients:

Ground pepper and coarse salt

1 1/2 1b of trimmed broccoli rabe

3 tbsp of pine nuts

1 tbsp of olive oil

1 tsp of lemon zest grated

Directions:

Cook broccoli rabe in a large pot of boiling salted water, until the color is bright green for 45 – 60 remove water from it and put aside.

Toast the pine nuts in the skillet over a medium heat, shake the skillet, until every part is golden brown for about 4 - 5 min; remove it from the skillet. Heat oil in the skillet and add the broccoli rabe; then cook, mixing it often, until thoroughly heated for about 3 - 5 min.

Mix the broccoli rabe with pine nuts and the lemon zest.

Season it with salt and pepper as desired.

Pan-Fried Beef Tenderloin

Ingredients:

2 tbsp of coarsely chopped rosemary (fresh)

2 tbsp of olive oil

1 tsp of kosher salt

1 tsp of grated lemon rind

2 garlic cloves, (minced)

4 (4-oz) beef tenderloin steaks (trimmed)

Directions:

Mix 2 tbsp of coarsely chopped rosemary (fresh), 2 tbsp of olive oil, 1tsp of kosher salt,1 tsp of grated lemon rind, 2 garlic cloves, (minced) in a small baking dish. Add steaks to marinade, turning to coat.

Cover and marinate steaks at room temperature one hour, turning occasionally.

Heat a cast-iron skillet over medium-high heat. Remove steaks from dish; dispose marinade, then place the steak in pan, then cook without interruption for 2 min or till steaks can be released easily from bottom of pan. Turn steaks over; cook for 2 min.

Turn steaks over, and cook for another 2 min or until your desire is got. Then leave it to stand 5 min.

Turkey skillet dinner

Prep time: 5mins

Cooking time: 25 minutes

Ingredients:

Non sticky cooking spray or

1/2 tbsp vegetable oil

¾ pound lean turkey (ground)

1 medium onion (peeled and chopped)

3 tomatoes (chopped)

3 Tablespoons of tomato paste

1 tsp each of dried basil, garlic powder and oregano

1 /4 teaspoon of black pepper

1/2 teaspoon of salt

2 medium zucchini (sliced)

Directions:

1. Spray non sticky cooking spray inside a big skillet.

2. Brown the turkey and onion over a medium heat until it is cooked thoroughly and onion becomes soft, for 10 min

3. Put in the tomatoes, tomato paste, and the seasonings. Allow to simmer over a medium heat for 10 minutes (bubble slowly)

4. Add zucchini and cook for 5 min more.

5. Add ground black pepper.

Turkey Breast Roast with Garlic, Paprika and black pepper

Cooking time: 4h 30min

Ingredients:

1. 5 lb -2 lb whole turkey breast half

4-5 garlic cloves

1 tablespoon of ground black pepper

3 tablespoons of paprika

2-3 tablespoons of olive oil and Black Pepper as desired

Directions:

1. Fill in a pot with enough water to cover the turkey breast completely, put salt as desired; put the turkey breast in leave it for about 2 hours in a cool place:

2. Combine ground black pepper with paprika in a bowl then add the olive oil and mix.

3. Peel the garlic cloves and slice them lengthwise into wedges:

4. Dry the turkey breast with paper towel and arrange it in the baking pan and stuff it with garlic wedges from top and bottom (create in holes with a small thin knife and stick garlic wedges in).

5. Spread the black pepper and paprika on the turkey breast and mix evenly from all sides:

6. Heat oven up to 485 F. Put in the baking pan into the oven for about 15 minutes, then turn oven off and leave it to roast for about 2 hours, leave the door closed till the scheduled time.

7. Then remove pan from the oven, slice meat up:

Cover the pan and cook the eggs, check regularly till the desired result is got (3-5 min for soft-set yolks, 7 - 9 min for hard-set yolks).

Top the bean mixture and eggs with the croutons.

Skillet Orecchiette with Sausage and Broccoli Rabe

Ingredients:

1 tbsp of olive oil

1 1b of pork sausage or spicy Italian-style chicken

1 1b of broccoli rabe, remove coarse stems and leaves coarsely chopped

2 minced or grated or cloves garlic, (about 2 tsps)

A pinch of red pepper flakes (if desired)

4 cups of store-bought or homemade low sodium chicken broth

3 cups of whole wheat or regular dried Orecchiette

Kosher salt and ground black pepper (freshly)

2 tbsp of freshly squeezed juice plus 1 tsp zest from 1 lemon

½ cup of grated Parmesan cheese (1 oz)

Store-bought or Homemade breadcrumbs

Directions:

1. Heat the oil in a 12-inch skillet over a medium-high heat until it shimmers. Then add the sausage then cook, until the color changes (break it apart) for about 3 - 4 min.

2. Put the sausage into a plate then add the broccoli rabe and sauté until it just begins to wilt for 2 min. Put it into the plate with the sausage. Remove all but 1 tbsp of fat. Add the garlic and the pepper flakes (optional) then cook, mixing continually until its nice odor comes out, for about 30 seconds.

3. Put in the broth use a wooden spoon to scrap up any browned traces from the bottom of the pan.

4. Add the pasta and check the heat as to keep up the strong and active bubbles. Cook until it becomes averagely tender for about 7 - 9 min maintains active bubbles in the liquid.

5. Return the broccoli rabe and the sausage to the pan then continue the cooking (mixing frequently to prevent the pasta from sticking to the pan) until pasta is fully cooked and broccoli is soft, for about 3 min

6. Remove it from the heat, season with salt and pepper as desired, and mix in the lemon juice and the zest. Mix in the cheese.

Top it with the breadcrumbs in a plate. Ready to eat

One- Skillet Bean & Broccoli Rabe Supper

Cooking time: 45 min

Ingredients:

3 slices of whole-wheat country bread (5-6 oz) remove the crusts

2 tbsp plus 1 tsp of extra-virgin olive oil (divided)

Freshly ground pepper to taste

4 oz of lamb merguez sausage, or Italian chicken, turkey or pork sausage links

2 cloves garlic, (thinly sliced)

1 bunch of broccoli rabe (about 12 oz) (trimmed and coarsely chopped)

2 cups of cooked cannellini beans, plus 1/2 of cup bean-cooking liquid or water

1/8 tsp of salt, plus a pinch (divided)

4 large eggs

Directions:

1. Firstly, Preheat the oven to 400° F.

2. Cut the bread into 1/2 to 1 inch irregular pieces.

3. Place on a large baking sheet and mix it with one tbsp of oil.

4. Season with pepper and bake until golden brown and crisp for about 10 - 12 min.

5. Then heat one tsp of oil in a large cast iron skillet over medium heat.

6. Take away sausage from the casing and cook, breaking it up, until browned and cooked thoroughly, for about 3 - 5 min.

7. Drain it on paper towels and allow the pan cool.

8. Remove any oil left in the pan, add the remaining one tbsp of oil and place over medium heat.

9. Then put in the garlic and cook, mixing continually, till fragrant, for about 30 sec.

10. Add broccoli rabe and cook, stirring, until weak and tender but still bright green, four to six minutes. (Add 1- 2 tbsp of water to have it wet if the greens seem dry)

11. Add beans, bean-cooking liquid (or water), the sausage and 1/8 tsp of salt to the pan, mix them. Bring to a simmer.

12. Create four spaces or holes in the bean mixture and break an egg into each one. Season the eggs with the remaining pinch of salt and pepper as desire.

Skillet Beef Stew

Ingredients:

2 tbsp of cooking oil

2 lb of beef stew meat, (1-inch cubes)

2 tsp of dried crushed thyme or oregano,

6 medium carrots, (peeled and quartered)

4 stalks celery, (2-inch lengthwise)

2 medium onions (1/2-inch slices)

6 cups of beef broth lower-sodium

1/3 cup of all-purpose flour

1 recipe Potato Mashers

Potato Mashers:

8 Yukon gold potatoes (about 23 pounds)

1 cup of milk

1/2 tsp of salt

1/2 tsp of black pepper

Directions:

Allow the beef turn brown in hot oil over a medium-high heat with the thyme and 1/4 tsp each of salt and pepper to taste all in 12-inch skillet. Take it away from the heat and set aside. Put in the carrots, the celery, and the onions into the skillet, cook and mix it for about 5 min. Return the beef to the skillet.

Mix the broth and the flour in a bowl; pour it into the skillet. Then bring it to boiling then low heat.

Simmer and cover for about 45 min. Remove the lid and simmer for 10 min or until the meat is soft.

Potato Mashers

Use a microwave-safe bowl micro cook the potatoes, bits by bits half, on a high power for 8 min, cover the bowl with a vented microwave-safe plastic wrap. Mash the potatoes with some milk, the salt, and then black pepper together.

Broccoli Rabe and Chicken Sandwich Recipe

Ingredients:

1 Bunch of Broccoli Rabe (washed, trimmed and cut)

2 (4 ounces each) thinly pounded Pieces of Chicken Breast

2 Tablespoons of Olive Oil, with extra teaspoon

2 chopped Cloves of Garlic

1 Clove of Garlic grated or minced finely

1 Small Sprig of Rosemary Fresh, chopped finely

1 Tablespoon of Balsamic Vinegar

1 Ball of sliced Fresh Mozzarella

Pinch of flakes Hot Pepper

Salt and Pepper, as desired

2 Focaccia or Roll Crusty Italian Rolls

Directions:

1) Mix the oil and the garlic in an average skillet then preheat it over a medium heat, when the garlic becomes good and lightly golden, put in a pinch of flakes hot pepper then cook for 30 seconds. Mix the broccoli rabe and cover the skillet for about a minute.

2) Pour about ½ cup of water, seasoning with the salt and pepper as desire cook them for about 8 - 10 min or till it is properly cooked and very soft.

3) Then prepare your chicken by soaking it in the balsamic vinegar, the finely minced garlic, the rosemary and the salt and pepper to taste then put it aside.

4) Transfer them to a plate and put the same skillet back on the stove and add in about one teaspoon of oil, let it preheat for about 3 - 4 min on each side or until fully cooked thoroughly.

5) While in the skillet, put in the broccoli rabe on the top of the chicken breast and top that with sliced mozzarella. Cover the skillet to allow the cheese to melt.

And can be served on crusty Italian roll

Beef and Vegetable Skillet

Preparation time: 10 min

Cooking time: 20 min

Ingredients:

1 package of Imagine Organic Culinary Simmer Sauce in Portobello

Red Wine

1 tbsp of olive oil

1 1b of sirloin tips (cubed)

7-8 small yellow potatoes halved

2 cups of baby carrots

1 cup of grape tomatoes

1 cup of baby Portobello mushrooms

Rosemary for garnish (fresh)

Directions:

Allow the carrots and potatoes to steam until almost nearly fork tender for about ten minutes and put it aside.

Heat the oil in large skillet over medium/high heat and add the steak tips and brown each side of the meat.

Cook it for three minutes on each side. Cook the meat to be nearly done through.

Add simmer sauce packet and vegetables to the skillet and mix to combine. Allow to simmer on low heat for five to seven minutes until hot and bubbles. Serve and Garnish with rosemary (if desire).

Easy Pan-Roasted Chicken Breasts with Bourbon-Mustard Pan Sauce

Ingredients;

2 whole airline chicken breasts or boneless skin-on chicken breasts (6 to 8 ounces each)

Kosher salt and ground black pepper (freshly)

1 tbsp of canola oil

3/4 cup of homemade or store-bought low-sodium chicken stock

1 1/2 tsp of powdered gelatin

1 small shallot, minced (about one tbsp)

1/4 cup of bourbon

2 tbsp of whole grain mustard

2 tbsp of unsalted butter

2 tsp of soy sauce

1 tsp of fresh juice from 1 lemon

1 tbsp of minced parsley leaves (fresh)

Directions:

1. Preheat oven to 450°F. Pat the chicken breasts dry and season very well with salt and pepper. Then heat the oil in

an oven-safe medium stainless steel skillet over a high heat till just starting to smoke.

Be careful as you lay the chicken breasts into hot skillet skin side down. Allow the chicken skin to be deep golden brown and very crisp before moving it for about six min. Flip the chicken breasts and transfer the skillet to the oven.

2. Meanwhile as the chicken roasts, add stock to a liquid measuring cup and sprinkle gelatin over it, put aside.

3. Cook the chicken until an instant-read thermometer inserted into the thickest part of the chicken breasts registers 150°F, for about 7 - 12 min. Take away skillet from oven and transfer chicken to a platter for cutting. Put aside to cool while you make the pan sauce.

4. Pour off all but one tbsp of fat from the skillet and place over high heat. Add shallots and cook, stirring, until softened and fragrant for about thirty seconds. Add bourbon and cook, scraping up any browned bits from the bottom of the pan with a wooden spoon, till reduced by half of the initial size, about one minute.

5. Add mustard and stock/gelatin mixture, cook on high heat till the sauce is reduced by about 2/3 for about 5 to 8 min. Mix in the butter, soy sauce, lemon juice and cook at a hard boil until emulsified, for about thirty seconds. Take away from heat and put aside.

6. Slice the chicken breasts into pieces and serve into plates.

Mix in the parsley into the pan sauce and season with salt and pepper to taste as desire, Spoon sauce over the chicken.

Pasta e Ceci

Preparation time: 10 minutes

Cooking time: 20 minutes

Ingredients:

2 tbsp of unsalted butter

2 tbsp of extra virgin olive oil

1 medium of (finely diced) sweet onion

1 large carrot (peeled and sliced into rounds)

3 garlic cloves (minced)

2 tbsp of tomato paste

1/2 tsp of oregano (dried)

1/2 tsp of thyme (dried)

1 (15 oz) can chickpeas (rinsed, drained)

6 cups of low sodium vegetable (chicken broth if preferred)

Salt and black pepper (freshly/ground)

2 cups of ditalini pasta (dried)

1/2 cup of Parmesan cheese (grated)

Directions:

Melt the butter and the olive oil in a large pot, over a medium heat, sauté onion, the carrot, and the garlic till it is soft, for five minutes. Season it with salt and pepper as desired.

Then add tomato paste, the oregano, the thyme, chickpeas, and 2 cups of the veggie broth; mix together. Boil them in the pot, then reduce heat and simmer gently for about five minutes.

Put in the remaining veggie broth, then boil it and cook the pasta in soup until just al dente, stirring continually to avoid it sticking together for ten minutes. Taste it and if need be for extra salt and pepper to be added do so. Mix in the Parmesan cheese.

Serve and spread a little more of the Parmesan on top of it.

Beef and Vegetable Skillet

Preparation time: 10 min

Cooking time: 20 min

Ingredients:

1 package of Imagine Organic Culinary Simmer Sauce in Portobello

Red Wine

1 tbsp of olive oil

1 1b of sirloin tips (cubed)

7-8 small yellow potatoes halved

2 cups of baby carrots

1 cup of grape tomatoes

1 cup of baby Portobello mushrooms

Rosemary for garnish (fresh)

Directions:

Allow the carrots and potatoes to steam until almost nearly fork tender for about ten minutes and put it aside.

Heat the oil in large skillet over medium/high heat and add the steak tips and brown each side of the meat.

Cook it for three minutes on each side. Cook the meat to be nearly done through.

Add simmer sauce packet and vegetables to the skillet and mix to combine. Allow to simmer on low heat for five to seven minutes until hot and bubbles. Serve and Garnish with rosemary (if desire).

One-Pan Orecchiette with Chickpeas and Olives

Ingredients:

12 oz of orecchiette

1 can (15.5 oz) of drained and rinsed) chickpeas

1/2 cups of Kalamata olives (remove the pits)

2 tbsp of tomato paste

3 cloves garlic (thinly sliced)

1 6-inch of sprig rosemary

3 tbsp of extra-virgin olive oil (with reserve to serve)

1/4 tsp of flakes red-pepper (with reserve to serve)

Coarse salt and freshly ground pepper

1/2 cup of grated Parmigiano-Reggiano (1 1/2 oz),

2 cups of baby arugula (2 oz)

Directions:

Mix the pasta, the chickpeas, the olives, the tomato paste, the clove garlic, the rosemary, oil and pepper flakes, and about 5 cups water in a large skillet.

Season it with salt and pepper very well. Then boil and cook it over a medium-high heat, mixing it occasionally till the pasta is al dente and the liquid is reduced in size to a sauce and coats the pasta for about 12 to 15 min

Take away the skillet from heat, dispose rosemary, and stir in the cheese.

More water can be added, a few tbsp at a time, to thin sauce (if desire).

Serve the pasta and arugula in your plate then drizzle the oil and sprinkle the cheese and pepper flakes as desired.

Chicken Spinach Roulade

Preparation time: 0 min

Cooking time: 0 min

Total time: 0 min

Ingredients:

(2) 4 to 6 oz chicken breasts, pounded and cut to ¼-inch thick

1 Tbsp of grape seed oil

¼ cup of pecans or walnuts

¼ cup of feta

¼ cup of diced sun-dried tomatoes

4 cups of baby spinach, fresh

¼ cup of shredded mozzarella, finely

1 medium of sliced onion

1 tbsp of olive oil

2 tsp of balsamic vinegar

1 tsp of hot sauce

Salt and pepper as desired

Directions:

Grind the feta, the pecans and the sun-dried tomatoes into the paste.

Sprinkle the mixture on the chicken breasts reserving about a ½ inch on all the sides. Put a layer of spinach.

Top it with the shredded mozzarella.

Tightly roll it and then tuck it in the ends. Bake the seam side down for about 30 min and the internal temperature is 160.

As the chicken cooks, prepare the topping.

Heat 1 tbsp of olive oil over a medium heat. Put the onions and then cook for about 3 to 4 min. put the spinach, the garlic, the balsamic vinegar and the hot sauce. Cook it till the spinach wilts and the garlic softened for about 2 to 3 minutes.

Top the chicken with the spinach mixture.

Creole Rice Skillet with Andouille Sausage

Serves: 4

Ingredients:

1-2 tbsp of lard or grass-fed butter

1 chopped onion

1 chopped bell pepper

2 cups of cooked rice

4 cooked and chopped andouille sausage links

1½ cups or 1 drained and rinsed can of red kidney beans

1 tsp of salt

1 tsp of black pepper

1 tsp of onion powder

2 tsp of garlic powder

1 tbsp of paprika

¼ tsp of cayenne pepper or red pepper flakes (or both)

1 tsp of oregano

1 tsp of thyme

Directions:

Heat the lard or the butter in a cast iron skillet over a medium heat. Sauté the onion and the bell pepper till they start to soften.

Put the rice, the sausage and the red beans. Mix and allow it cook till it is warmed thoroughly.

Put the spices and mix till it is completely

Roasted Chili, Garlic & Lime Chicken Quesadillas

Preparation time: 10 min

Cooking time: 20 min

Ingredients:

1 tbsp of vegetable oil

1 1b of skinless boneless chicken breasts (thin strips)

1 medium bell pepper, sliced thinly

1 package of McCormick Fajita with Roasted Chili, Garlic & Lime Skillet Sauce

8 flour tortillas, 8 inches

2 cups of shredded Monterey Jack cheese

Directions:

1. Preheat the oven to 400°F. Heat oil in a large non sticky skillet on a medium-high heat.

2. Add the chicken, cook and stir it for about five minutes or till lightly browned.

3. Put in the vegetables and then cook and mix for about three minutes.

4. Mix in the Skillet Sauce. Lower the heat then simmer for three minutes or till the chicken is thoroughly cooked and vegetables tender-crisp. Pour evenly the tortillas on the 2 baking sheets. Spread each with 1/2 cup of shredded cheese then you can top it with a second tortilla.

5. Then bake for five to ten minutes or until the cheese is melted and tortillas are lightly browned.

Beef stew

Cooking time: 3h 35 minutes

Ingredients:

Olive oil

1 knob butter

1 onion (peeled and chopped)

1 handful of sage leaves (fresh)

800 g of quality stewing steak (cut into 5cm pieces)

Sea salt

Fresh black pepper (ground)

Dust with flour

2 parsnips (peeled and in quarter)

4 (peeled and halved) carrots

½ butternut squash (halved, remove seed and coarsely diced)

1 handful of Jerusalem artichokes, peeled and halved (as desire)

500 g of small potatoes

2 tbsp of tomato purée

½ bottle of red wine

285 ml of vegetable stock or organic beef

1 lemon zest (finely grated)

1 handful of Rosemary (leaves)

1 garlic clove (peeled and neatly chopped)

Directions:

1. Preheat the oven to 160ºC

2. Put in a little oil and the knob of butter into a right pot or casserole pan.

3. Add the onion and the fresh sage leaves and fry for about three to four minutes.

4. Mix the meat in a small quantity of seasoned flour, add it to the vegetables the tomato purée, the wine and stock in the pan and mix them together gently.

5. Season it very well with the fresh grounded black pepper and with a little salt.

6. Put a lid and boil and cook in the preheated oven until the meat is soft. It takes between three to four hours, the size of meat use will determine the time and how fresh it is. When you check a piece of the meat and it falls apart this indicates that it is done.

Then reduce the heat to about 110ºC ¼ and just hold it till you're ready to serve.

Stir in the lemon zest, rosemary (chopped) and garlic together and sprinkle it over the stew.

5-Minute Guacamole

Servings: 2-3 units

Preparation Time: 2 -3

Cooking time:5 minutes

Ingredients:

1 ripe avocado

1/2 tbsp of lime juice

1/4 tsp of garlic powder

1/4 tsp of onion powder

1/2 tsp of chili powder

1/2 teaspoon cumin, ground

1/4 tsp of kosher salt

1/2 tsp of cilantro, dried

1 dash dash cayenne pepper

To taste

1 roma tomato (seeded and diced)

Directions:

Chop and then scoop the avocado into a small bowl. Sprinkle the remaining ingredients apart from tomato.

Mash it with a fork till it slightly chunky.

Mix in the diced tomatoes. Check the lime and the salt as desired before you serve.

Home-style Beef Stew

Ingredients:

1 pound of beef eye round roast (1-inch pieces)

2 Tablespoons of all-purpose flour

2 Tablespoons of vegetable oil

2 medium onions (chopped)

2 garlic cloves (finely chopped)

1 tub Knorr Homestyle Stock – Beef (chopped)

2 cups of water

2 teaspoons of Worcestershire sauce

4 cups of red potatoes (baby) (halved)

3 sliced carrots

Directions:

1. Mix the beef with the flour and set aside.

2. Heat the oil in large skillet over medium heat and brown the beef.

3. Take away the beef from skillet and put aside.

4. Mix onions and garlic in the skillet and cook, mixing frequently, till the onions are soft for about 4 min.

5. Mix in the Knorr Homestyle Stock - (the numbers 6, 7, 8) and beef. Then boil over high heat, stirring till the Stock melts.

6. Then reduce the heat and simmer it covered, mixing occasionally, for about 40 min or till the beef is almost soft.

7. Mix in 9 and 10 ingredients and simmer for another 40 min or till the beef and vegetables are soft.

Spring Vegetable Skillet

Ingredients:

16 baby carrots with tops (10 ounce)

3/4 tsp of kosher salt (divided)

12 oz of sugar snap peas (trimmed)

1 1/2 tbsp of butter

1 tbsp of tarragon (chopped fresh)

1/4 tsp of black pepper (freshly ground)

1 tsp of grated lemon rind

1 tsp of lemon juice (fresh)

Directions:

1. Peel the carrots, and cut off the tops to within one inch of carrot; cut in half lengthwise.

2. Place 1/4 tsp of salt in a large skillet of water; and boil, add the carrots and peas then cook for tree minutes or until crisp-tender. Drain.

3. Melt the butter in a large nonstick skillet over medium-high heat. Add the vegetables, and cook for one minute, mixing it to coat.

4. Mix in the remaining 1/2 tsp of salt, tarragon, and pepper then cook for one minute.

Take it away from the heat; mix in the rind and juice.

Zucchini, Brie & Caramelized Onion Panini

Preparation time; 10 min

Cooking time: 15 min

Total time: 25 min

Serves: 2

Ingredients

4 slices of whole wheat sourdough bread

2 slices of Brie cheese

1 zucchini

½ small thinly sliced onion

1 tablespoon of olive oil

Pepper

Directions:

Preheat your indoor grill or panini, heat a skillet over a medium heat.

Heat the oil in a skillet on a medium-low.

Slice the zucchini into half, and then the lengthwise in thinly strips.

Cook the zucchini and the onions in your skillet for 5 minutes, till soft.

Put extra olive oil onto the slices of bread if desired, then put on top of the two slices the zucchini, the onions and the Brie. Spread with some pepper, and then close it with the other two slices and then press firmly together.

Put onto your grill or panini then press and close. Cook till it is crisp, for 4 minutes. Or, you put it onto a skillet and then put another skillet on the top of the sandwich, cook each side for some minutes till crispy and the Brie melts

Honey Sriracha Skillet Pork Chops

Preparation time: 5 min

Cooking time: 25 min

Total time: 30 min

Serves 4

Ingredients;

1 tbsp of coconut oil (enough to coat the pan)

4 large pork loin chops

Enough pinch black pepper

1 tbsp of quality honey

1 tbsp of Sriracha

Directions:

Preheat your oven to 350. Heat the coconut oil over a medium heat in the oven-proof skillet, cast iron skillet is preferred.

Season the chops with only pepper (salting it makes the dish taste salty) and then brown it in the skillet, for about 3-5 min for each side. The pork indicates its readiness when it can be easily released from the pan. let it continue the cooking if it does not release easily from the pot. It will release whenever it's browned and ready.

Put the honey and the Sriracha.

Transfer the skillet onto the oven and then bake till the pork is cooked throughly and the juices run clear, for 15 min.

Mix the juices on the bottom of your pan to stir the pork renderings, the coconut oil, the honey and the Sriracha together.

Serve it immediately. You can put some of the extra liquid on the top.

Refrigerate the leftovers in an airtight container for 5-7 days.

Chicken Barley Soup

Preparation time: 0 min

Cooking time: 0 min

Total time: 0 min

Ingredients:

3 cups of cooked chicken

1 cup of carrots, chopped

1 cup of celery, chopped

1 cup of onions, chopped

2 minced cloves garlic

8 cups of chicken stock

1 cup of quick cook barley

4 cups of arugula

1 Tbsp of olive oil

Directions:

Heat the stock. Sauté the carrots, the celery and the onion in the oil till crisp cooked. Put 2 cups of the stock and the garlic. Lower the heat and then simmer till your desired consistency is achieved. Put the vegetables into the stock pot.

While the vegetable is cooking, prepare the barley. Boil 2 cups of broth. Put the barley, then cover and then simmer for about 8 min.

Put the barley and the chicken into the stock and the vegetables. Put the arugula and then cook just till the arugula wilts (for 2 min).

Serve it alone or with the crusty bread or the crackers.

Paprika Chicken Salad

Ingredients

2 cups of chopped cooked chicken

¼ cup of chopped sun-dried tomatoes (in ½ cup water)

¼ cup of celery, chopped

2 tbsp of smoked almond pieces

1 tbsp of olive oil

1 tsp of red wine vinegar

⅛ Tsp of smoked paprika

½ tsp of honey

Salt to taste

Directions:

Soak in the tomatoes inside water for about 30 min. Drain and then reserve liquid.

Stir in the chicken, the tomatoes, the celery, and the almonds together.

Whisk the vinegar, the oil, the paprika, the honey and the salt together in a separate bowl.

Put the dressing to the chicken mixture. Put some of the reserved water to moisten it as desired

Shaved Beet & Carrot Salad with Spicy-Sweet Dressing

Ingredients:

1 large beet

4 large carrots

3/4 cup of kefir vinegar (apple cider vinegar or can sub pineapple)

1 large tomato

1.5 tablespoon of mango jam

1 ají dulce pepper

2" knob of turmeric

2 garlic cloves

1 teaspoon of salt

Directions:

Grate the beet and the carrots and put it aside

Mix all the remaining ingredients in a blender

Blend till it is smooth

Pour it over the beet/carrot salad and then mix.

Roasted Sweet Potato and Quinoa Soup

Preparation time: 15 minutes

Cooking time: 50 minutes

Ingredients:

1 large sweet potato

½ large sweet onions diced

2 carrots (diced)

1 large minced clove garlic

3 tbsp of olive oil, divided

Sea salt and pepper as desired

900 ml of vegetable stock or chicken

1 cup of cooked quinoa

1/2 cup of panko crumbs

1 tbsp of butter

1/3 cup of grated parmesan

Parsley for garnishing

Directions:

1. Pre-heat the oven to 400F.

2. Peel the large sweet potato, put the sweet potato on a baking sheet (trimmed) and slowly drop about two tablespoons of olive oil and the sea salt then roast them in the oven for about 20 minutes.

3. Sauté the onion and the carrot in a large pot until it is soft and add potato to the onion mixture then add the chicken stock. Simmer it for about 20-30 minutes till all vegetables are relatively soft.

4. Mix them with a blender thoroughly until pureed. Check your seasoning to your taste then add the quinoa and heat again.

5. If it is with panko topping, melt the butter in a fry pan and add panko and then cook until it becomes lightly brown.

6. Add parmesan and mix, top bowls of soup with panko crumbs and then garnish with the parsley.

Cast-Iron Carrots with Curry

Total Time: 35 min

Preparation: 25 min

Cooking time: 10 min

Yield: 4 servings

Ingredients:

3 tbsp of coconut oil

2 lb of peeled carrots, halved lengthwise and sliced on the bias 1-inch thickness

1/2 tsp of salt

1/2 tsp of black pepper, ground

1 tsp of curry powder

1/4 cup of coarsely chopped cilantro, fresh

Directions:

Heat a big heavy skillet over a medium-high heat and then put the coconut oil. When it is hot, put the carrots in an equal layer to maximize the contact with the pan. Spread with the salt and also pepper, and then fry the carrots, turning at intervals of 3 or 4 minutes, till they are dark caramelized brown in spots, for about 8 to 10 minutes.

Put the curry powder and then mix to have them combined. Sprinkle the cilantro on the top and then serve.

Skillet Chicken with Bacon and White Wine Sauce

Ingredients:

3 slices of bacon

½ cup of flour

Salt and pepper

2 tsp of herbes de Provence

1½ - 2 Pound of chicken thighs with skin

1-2 tbsp of olive oil

2 shallots (to be thinly sliced)

½ cup of white wine (dry)

1 cup of chicken stock

Dried or parsley (fresh) to top.

Directions:

BACON:

1. Preheat the oven to 350 degrees. Then heat a large cast iron skillet over a medium high heat.

2. Cut the bacon into small pieces then fry them for about five to six minutes, stirring it continually.

3. Take it away from the pan with a slotted spoon and put aside, leaving back hot bacon grease in pan (low the heat and prepare the chicken).

CHICKEN:

1. Toss flour with salt and pepper and the herbes de Provence. The pieces of the chicken dredged in the flour mixture and take them to the hot pan.

2. Pan-fry the chicken for some minutes on each side, till golden brown, should not be thoroughly cooked.

3. Take away the chicken from the pan and put it aside on plate.

SHALLOTS:

1. Add shallots to pan with the olive oil. Sauté 5-10 min, till softened, with sweet smell and golden brown.

2. Put in the wine gently, mixing to get all the browned bits from inside the pan.

3. Add chicken stock and cook till it reduces slightly for 5 to 10 min

BAKE:

1. Add chicken and bacon to the pan and bake for about 40 min, baste the chicken interval of ten or fifteen minutes with the pan sauce.

2. Take it away from oven when chicken skin is crispy and it is done (fully cooked).

3. Remove the oil on the top of the sauce if desire.

Pan-Seared Filet Mignon with Cabernet Sauce

Ingredients:

4 tbsp (1/2 stick) of chilled butter

4 filet mignon steaks (about 4 oz each)

1/3 cup of shallots (chopped)

2/3 cup of Cabernet Sauvignon

1 generous tbsp of capers (drained)

1 tbsp of Dijon mustard

1/3 cup of fresh parsley (chopped)

Directions:

1. One tbsp of butter is melted in heavy large skillet over a medium-high heat.

2. The two sides of the steaks are sprinkled with salt and enough of black pepper (ground).

3. Put it in the skillet then cook to your desire result for about four minutes for each side for medium.

4. Place the steaks into plates, tent with foil.

5. Inside the skillet melt one tbsp of butter over a medium-high heat.

6. Add the shallots; sauté one minute. Then add the wine, the capers, and the mustard; simmer until thickened, for about 2 min. Mix in the parsley.

Reduce the heat to a medium-low. Mix in the remaining 2 tbsp of butter.

Season sauce with salt and pepper (to taste).

Fajita with Roasted Chili Garlic and Lime Skillet Sauce

Preparation Time: 10 min

Cook Time: 15 min.

Ingredients:

Water, Spices (Roasted Chili Pepper, Paprika), Lime juice

Soy Sauce (Water, Wheat, Soybeans, Salt),

Modified Corn Starch, garlic, Sugar, Salt, Natural Flavor, Lactic Acid and Citric Acid.

1 pkg. of McCormick Skillet Sauce

1 tablespoon of vegetable oil

1 pound skinless and boneless and chicken breasts (in strips)

1 bell pepper and 1 onion (in strips)

8 flour tortillas

Directions:

HEAT the oil in a skillet on a medium-high heat. Put the chicken and then cook till browned then add vegetables, cook and mix for three minutes. Mix in the Sauce. Lower the heat then simmer for about three minutes, until the chicken is cooked thoroughly and the vegetables are soft-crisp. Serve it warm with topping if desired.

Steamed Oysters with Smokey Peach Sauce

16 appetizer servings

Ingredients:

For the sauce

1/4 cup of melted unsalted butter

2 cups of defrosted frozen peaches

2 Tbsp of smoked paprika

4 Tbsp of chopped Italian parsley for the oysters

1/2 bushel of oysters, fresh

Directions:

For the Smokey peach sauce

Take off the peaches from the freezer and then thaw. Put the slices of thawed peach in the blender and then puree.

Melt the butter in the sauce pan over a medium heat.

Put the peach puree and the smoked paprika. Cook for about 3 minutes, mixing often.

can be made several hours before you serve. Heat it again slowly and then put freshly chopped parsley before you serve.

For the oysters

Wash and then scrub oysters.

Fill a big stock pot with some inches of water. Then boil. Put the steamer basket into the pot.

Fill in the steamer basket with the oysters. Replace the lid on the pot and then cook till the shells open slightly.

Shuck the oysters carefully by removing the top shell. Put on the platter and then serve with the sauce.

END

Thank you for reading my book. If you enjoyed it, won't you please take a moment to look at my other titles?

Thanks!

Billy Dunklin

CPSIA information can be obtained
at www.ICGtesting.com
Printed in the USA
LVHW041637220620
658705LV00002B/473